Living Eucharist

The Transforming Presence of Christ

FR. JEFF VONLEHMEN

ONE LIGUORI DRIVE
LIGUORI MO 63057-9999

Imprimi Potest:
Richard Thibodeau, C.Ss.R.
Provincial, Denver Province
The Redemptorists

Imprimatur:
Most Reverend Michael J. Sheridan
Auxiliary Bishop, Archdiocese of St. Louis

ISBN 0-7648-0800-1
© 2002, Jeff VonLehmen
Printed in the United States of America
02 03 04 05 06   5 4 3 2 1

All rights reserved. No part of this booklet may be reproduced, stored in a retrieval system, or transmitted without the written permission of Liguori Publications.

Except where noted, Scripture quotations are from the *New Revised Standard Version of the Bible*, copyright © 1989 by the Division of Christian Education of the National Council of Churches of Christ in the USA. Used with permission. All rights reserved.

The opinion piece "Is Jesus Weeping over Cincinnati?" is reprinted with permission of the author.

Contents

Introduction / 5

DOORWAY ONE:
Transformation of Death into Life / 7

DOORWAY TWO:
Real Reverence Is Living the Eucharist / 15

DOORWAY THREE:
Real Presence / 26

The Holy Spirit Is Our Doorkeeper / 34

ADDENDUM:
A Few Common Questions from Youth and Young Adults / 45

*In loving memory of my father,
Louis VonLehmen,
who went to Mass daily, praying for his
family and for the world*

Introduction

We need help with the richest gift of divine love that Jesus wishes to give us: the Eucharist! We do not need help so much in order to get more *out of* Mass, but to get more *into* it.

The following reflections offer three "doorways" into the Eucharist—the celebration of the paschal mystery—through which we can spiritually walk in order to get more into it. The three doorways lead us to places at the heart of Jesus and the heart of the Eucharist which concern our pain (Doorway One: Transformation of Death into Life), our relationships (Doorway Two: Real Reverence Is Living the Eucharist), and our presence to God who is with us (Doorway Three: Real Presence).

These reflections have developed as a result of my experiences with youth, young adults, and strangely enough, their grandparents. Together we have discovered the richness of Christ's greatest treasure and three doorways through which to enter.

DOORWAY ONE

Transformation of Death into Life

One Sunday morning, a woman by the name of Sara stood up in front of the congregation to give a talk on lay ministry. She had suffered from breast cancer and undergone a mastectomy. She knew the pain of sickness, so she decided to become a lay minister for the sick in the parish. Sara talked about how her sickness had become something life-giving. The horror of cancer and the humiliation of having her breast removed had become the inspiration for serving others in their sickness and a source of life for them as well as for Sara. The transformation of sickness and death into life is one doorway into the mystery of the Eucharist.

As we enter this doorway, we notice an important image, the Lamb, which will help us understand the transformation of death into life. The Hebrew word for lamb is *pasch*, the root meaning of the Passover and paschal mystery. The image of the Lamb is used throughout the eucharistic celebration. During the

Gloria, we sing, "Lord God, Lamb of God, you take away the sin of the world." Just before communion, the congregation proclaims three times: "Lamb of God, you take away the sins of the world." In the Scriptures, we find in Paul's First Letter to the Corinthians a reference to Jesus as the Passover lamb (1 Corinthians 5:7). In John's Gospel, John the Baptist refers to Jesus as the "Lamb of God who takes away the sins of the world" (John 1:29). The time of Jesus' death is situated during the Passover. The words spoken during the Lord's Supper, "This is my body which will be given up for you…this is the cup of my blood…shed for you" (see Mark 14:22-24, Luke 22:19-20, Matthew 26:26-28), is paschal language referring to the Passover Lamb.

The lamb has its ties to the Exodus. At the beginning of the Exodus, the Hebrews were to slaughter a firstborn male lamb, put its blood on the doorpost and consume the meat. The angel of death then passed over each home with the lamb's blood on the doorpost. The sacrifice of the lamb is connected to being freed from the slavery in Egypt. Since slavery is considered a kind of death in itself, freedom from slavery is robbing death of its power. The death of the lamb effects the death of death (slavery). The result is freedom and life.

But why a lamb? Why not a turkey? Here is an important insight about the paschal lamb. The lamb signifies more than simply physical freedom and life. The lamb may have been a taboo animal in ancient Egypt. That is to say, the animal was considered sacred and associated with the gods of ancient Egypt.

The sacred lamb was not to be sacrificed and eaten, but reverenced as an animal god. So, for the Hebrews, to sacrifice the lamb meant sacrificing idolatry and false worship. The sacrifice of the lamb meant the death of death (idolatry) which is life with God—not merely physical life.

It is no wonder, then, that in John's passion narrative, Jesus dies on the cross at exactly the time the lambs are being slain in the Temple for the Passover. Jesus' death is the death of death (sin and its consequences). The meaning of the sacrifice of the Lamb, Jesus, as the death of death is expressed in several of Paul's letters:

We know that Christ, being raised from the dead, will never die again; death no longer has dominion over him.

ROMANS 6:9

For our sake he made him to be sin who knew no sin, so that in him we might become the righteousness of God.

2 CORINTHIANS 5:21

What then are we to say about these things? If God is for us, who is against us? He who did not withhold his own Son, but gave him up for all of us, will he not with him also give us everything else? Who will bring any charge against God's elect? It is God who justifies.

Who is to condemn? It is Christ Jesus, who died, yes, who was raised, who is at the right hand of God, who indeed intercedes for us. Who will separate us from the love of Christ? Will hardship, or distress, or persecution, or famine, or nakedness, or peril, or sword? As it is written, "For your sake we are being killed all day long; we are accounted as sheep to be slaughtered." No, in all these things we are more than conquerors through him who loved us. For I am convinced that neither death, nor life, nor angels, nor rulers, nor things present, nor things to come, nor powers, nor height, nor depth, nor anything else in all creation, will be able to separate us from the love of God in Christ Jesus our Lord.

ROMANS 8:31-39

Sara's life is witness to this paschal mystery in which she fully participates every Sunday with the community. Death in the form of cancer has lost its power over her. Instead of the cancer destroying her mentally, emotionally, and spiritually, she uses it to better the lives of those in her family and parish as a minister to the sick. This transformation does not happen overnight. The Eucharist and paschal mystery are not magic. The effects of the Lamb of God, the "death of death," takes effect in us slowly over a period of time as we consciously connect our pain with the passion of Jesus and participate communally at the eucharistic table where death has been transformed into life.

What a gift this is! How many people, young and old, think they have nowhere to go with pain—pain in a relationship, pain of injustice and violence, illness, loss, loneliness, sexual problems, an intense feeling of emptiness, etc.? How many of us feel as though our wounded past or world controls us and still has power over us? Yet, here at the eucharistic table we enter a doorway that transforms pain and death into life with Christ, so that destructive powers have no more power over us.

There are further examples that demonstrate the power of the paschal mystery to turn pain into life and to reveal the difference between sacrifice and suffering.

One New Year's Eve, a young woman was brutally raped and murdered. Her name was Carlie Schulenberg. This violent loss inflicted unbelievable pain upon Carlie's sister, Kim, her parents Connie and Bob, her stepparents, and her grandmother. All Kim kept saying to herself at the time of the funeral Mass was: "He [the rapist] was the last one to touch her." During the funeral Mass itself, Connie could hardly even make it down the aisle into her seat without passing out. Bob wanted the murderer to "fry" in hell. During the liturgy, a love more powerful than death began to take root. Christ's love, which was victorious in his own passion and death, became more present through the gathering of the community and in the breaking of the bread. Kim began to experience that it was really the gentle hand of God that last touched Carlie. Bob began to move from hatred to forgiveness (although this would take a long time—the Eucharist works slowly on us). Bob began to take part in the RCIA to renew his faith and continue to experience the power of Christ's love over pain with the faithful at the eucharistic table. Connie found that coming to prayer and Mass helped her tremendously. She expressed it this way:

> "I am trying to give my pain to God. It is not the same as relief. It is letting go. I have no control over Carlie's life or her death. I am not going to let her pain control me. The gathering of people at Mass was a good place for that. It might be the only place. While not understanding the paschal mystery, my experience of it helps me to let go of the pain. I am starting to experience God. If Christ is willing to take our pain, everyone's pain, because he accepted the pain of the cross, why not bring it to him together with others at Mass, not just giving the pain to the wind, but giving it to Christ? I guess letting go of the pain is a kind of forgiveness for the man who murdered Carlie."

This is truly the experience of the paschal mystery as the "death of death" in Christ's passion, death, and resurrection.

Here again we see that the transformation of death into life does not happen magically or instantly. There is sacrifice involved. However, there is a difference between sacrifice and suffering. Suffering in itself is pure pain. Sacrifice brings life and unity. Kim sacrificed the negative thought that the rapist was the last one to touch her sister for the positive truth that "the gentle hand of God touched her last." Bob sacrificed his wish for capital punishment for Christian forgiveness and justice. Connie was willing to sacrifice her need to control for "letting go" by surrendering it to the love of the Lord on the cross with the prayerful support of the community at Mass. The result was more life and freedom. Suffering is pure hell, pain without love. Sacrifice is what we do when we unite ourselves with Jesus who is love.

Turn again to the image of the Lamb of God or the blood of the Lamb. In the Hebrew mentality, life resides in the blood. It is only God who can give life. So through blood, God is giving life to the creature. In the Hebrew Scriptures, when the sacrifice of a Passover lamb occurs or the sacrifice of lambs for atonement are offered, the sprinkling of the blood is a way of saying: "Let God's life take hold of our lives again, so we can live in the freedom of God's people." When we partake of the Eucharist, the body and blood of the Passover Lamb, we are allowing God's life to take hold of our life so that we know that God's love "rules" our life, not our pain or wounded selves.

It is important to understand that the transformation of death into life involves sacrifices of love and not more suffering. There is a thought that goes something like this: "The more you suffer, the closer you are to heaven." The truth is that everyone in the world suffers, from Adam and Eve to Pope John Paul II, from Adolf Hitler to Mother Teresa. Does that mean everyone is going to heaven just because they suffer? There is a difference between suffering and sacrifice. The suffering and passion of Jesus is always put into the context of sacrificial love: "No one has greater love than this, to lay down one's life for one's friends" (John 15:13).

The paschal mystery is the transformation of death into life and the transformation of suffering into a sacrifice of love. United through the paschal mystery with the love Jesus showed in his passion, we can turn into good everything that evil seeks to destroy. The language of body and blood, the cross, the sacrifice of the Mass, and symbols such as the crucifix and the lamb are not simply about suffering and death, but about the "death of death," which is life with Christ. It is no wonder the cross is shaped like a plus sign. It is a positive in our life, not a negative.

DOORWAY TWO

Real Reverence Is Living the Eucharist

If we treasure a friendship, we enter more fully into the friendship. When we revere a gift, we enter more deeply into the gift. Likewise, reverence for the Eucharist is to enter more fully into our relationship with God and with each other. Reverence is not a matter of acting "holier than thou." Consider the following examples. A teenage girl went to Mass every Sunday with her family. The family sat right up front. They folded their hands just right, genuflected perfectly, dressed formally, and received communion on the tongue. People spoke of how reverent the family was during Mass. What people did not know was that the father verbally, mentally, and emotionally abused the teenager severely on a regular basis. It was a case of domestic violence, a terrible family secret. On the other hand, one day a woman came late to the Saturday evening Mass wearing a sweat suit. Her hair was a mess and she looked unkept. She was accused of being irreverent. The truth was she had just spent the last twenty-four hours in the hospital with a sick child. She was on the way home to pick up a few things and thought she would make the evening Mass before she rushed back to the hospital. Now, who was really reverent, the mother in the sweat suit or the people criticizing her? Was the abusive father who did everything "liturgically correct" really reverent? Reverence is not the exterior display of a posture, a pose, or a set of clothes. It is not the etiquette we observe. Reverence is how well we relate to God and to one another. Daily reverence for those for whom Christ died (all people) fosters a true spirit of reverence of Christ at the eucharistic table. Reverence is the action of living the Eucharist daily. This appears to be the meaning of reverence offered by the early Christians and by Jesus himself.

Listen to Ignatius of Antioch (second century):

People hold a strange doctrine of touching the grace of Jesus Christ (receiving communion) if they have no care for charity, none for the widow, none for the orphan, none for the afflicted, none for the prisoner, none for the hungry or thirsty.

LETTER TO THE SMYRNEANS, CHP. VI

In other words, Ignatius is saying that you can't just show up at Mass, act as though you are reverently receiving communion, and hope to get something out of it. We live the Eucharist daily in our relationships by our charity, our care for the widow, the orphan, etc. True reverence is *living* the Eucharist.

How about going back even a little earlier, to the time of the apostle Paul?

When you come together as a church, I hear that there are divisions among you; and to some extent I believe it. Indeed, there have to be factions among you, for only so will it become clear who among you are genuine. When you come together, it is not really to eat the Lord's supper. For when the time comes to eat, each of you goes ahead with your own supper, and one goes hungry and another becomes drunk. What! Do you not have homes to eat and drink in? Or do you show contempt for the church of God and humiliate those who have nothing?

1 Corinthians 11:18-22

Reverence shows itself in how we treat one another. Jesus himself decided what reverence is:

He said to them, "Then do you also fail to understand? Do you not see that whatever goes into a person from outside cannot defile, since it enters, not the heart but the stomach, and goes out into the sewer?" (Thus he declared all foods clean.) And he said, "It is what comes out of a person that defiles. For it is from

> *within, from the human heart, that evil intentions come: fornication, theft, murder, adultery, avarice, wickedness, deceit, licentiousness, envy, slander, pride, folly. All these evil things come from within, and they defile a person."*
>
> MARK 7:18-23

It is what comes from within you that makes you reverent or not and fundamentally makes worship authentic or not. Reverence is fundamentally internal and relational, not simply external appearances or superficial behavior. Notice that Christ's list of evils is what destroys relationships.

Real reverence is relational. It has to do with how we relate to one another before we gather for Eucharist and after we leave. Jesus says:

> *So when you are offering your gift at the altar, if you remember that your brother or sister has something against you, leave your gift there before the altar and go; first be reconciled to your brother or sister, and then come and offer your gift.*
>
> MATTHEW 5:23-24

Reverence means living the Eucharist daily with the divine love, grace, and life ("death of death") we receive while taking from the cup and breaking the bread together: reconciling and transforming our relationships before we arrive on Sunday and after we leave the altar following the end of Mass. Reverence is relational. Once you learn to live the Eucharist, you will never again be bored at Mass.

What does a young, twenty-three-year-old woman have to say about all this? Her name is Julie Kalker and her short life has plenty to say. It might be well at this point to share the story of Julie's reverence. Julie had an exceptional love for the Eucharist. In the salutatory address she gave at her high school graduation from Villa Madonna Academy, she said: "What lies behind us, and what lies before us are tiny matters compared to what lies within us…and what is within us comes from the faculty, the sharing and planning of the liturgy, the friendships…the ability to accept people's differences and the realization that God is present in our lives." In college, Julie loved to join the community at the eucharistic table. Why? Where did this love come from? What had she discovered at such a young age? She had found the secret in living the Eucharist. When you live the Eucharist, it begins to live in you. In giving her life for others, Julie experienced Jesus giving his life away to her and the world in the paschal mystery.

When Julie became a schoolteacher, she took under her care a little Latina girl from a poor immigrant family in order to help the child learn English. One of Julie's favorite quotes was called *If I Could:*

If I Could

If I could, I would teach each child
 to be positive,
 to smile, to love, and be loved.
If I could, I would teach each child
 to take time
 to observe some miracle of nature—
 the song of a bird, the beauty
 of a snowflake,
 the orange glow of a winter sunset.
If I could, I would teach each child to feel
 warmly about
 the peers for whom the task of
 learning does not come easily.
If I could, I would teach each one to be kind
 to all living creatures and to crowd
 out of their lives
 feelings of guilt, misunderstanding,
 and lack of compassion.
If I could, I would teach each child that
 it is okay to show their feelings by
 laughing, crying,
 or touching someone they
 care about.
Every day I would have each child feel
 special and,
 through my actions, each one
 would know
 how much I really care.

A hundred years from now, nobody will
  remember who I was,
what I did, or how much money I
  had; but the world
may be a little different and a
  little better
because I was important in the life
  of a child.

AUTHOR UNKNOWN

Julie gave part of her life for the little girl by being important in her life. Having the experience of giving her life for another, Julie could more clearly experience Jesus giving his life to us and for us in the breaking of the bread.

The day came when Julie had to move back home to live with her parents because she discovered she had cancer. But as much as her body was riddled with cancer, she still struggled down the aisle at Mass on Sunday to be with the people in prayer and worship. It meant so much to her because of what she experienced from living the Eucharist. The Thursday before she died, she wished to have a Mass at home—totally reconciled with God, her family, friends, and community. It was truly a powerful experience of a young lady who revealed to us a doorway into the paschal mystery: Real reverence is living the Eucharist.

What has been revealed by Jesus, the early Christians, Church history, as well as the life of a young adult, Julie Kalker, is this: Good Eucharist is a right relationship with God and each other; it is becoming what we receive, Christian in our daily actions. Good liturgy does not make good Eucharist. Good relationships make good Eucharist. Good Eucharist makes good liturgy. Live the Eucharist.

Living with a preferential option for the poor and the defenseless, including the unborn, elderly, and handicapped, are all examples of living the Eucharist with true reverence. To focus on reverence as a way of living the Eucharist brings healing to our society and world. Martin Luther King, Jr. said it well:

> *"A religion true to its nature must also be concerned about [human] social conditions. Any religion that professes to be concerned with [human souls] and is not concerned with the slums that damn them, the economic conditions that strangle them, and the social conditions that cripple them, is a dry as dust religion."*
>
> INSCRIPTION AT
> THE MARTIN LUTHER KING
> NATIONAL HISTORIC SITE,
> ATLANTA, GEORGIA.

Also, reverence as a way of living the Eucharist may bring healing within the Church. Too often, Catholics make a mockery of the Church by arguments over liturgical preferences (Latin Mass vs. English Mass, gold chalice vs. wood chalice, simple garments vs. elaborate garments, etc). I have great respect for our older Catholics and for our older priests. One such priest became increasingly upset over the arguments over liturgical preferences. So, he wrote the following opinion piece in the *Catholic Telegraph*, the paper of the Archdiocese of Cincinnati.

Is Jesus Weeping over Cincinnati?

I am a Cincinnati priest, 77 years of age. I am quite saddened at the controversy going on in our Archdiocese. In the Scriptures, we know of two times that Jesus wept during his public ministry: at the tomb of his friend Lazarus who had died, and on a hillside outside Jerusalem when he realized that many of the people for whom he was soon to be crucified would not accept his message of love, peace, and unity. Warm tears flowed down his cheeks.

I have been privileged to travel to a hundred countries, primarily to study the Church's role in poverty problems. I have smelled many open sewers and have seen the extended bellies of many, many babies who didn't even own their own pair of shoes. I know that millions of infants are being aborted each year, mainly in the rich countries; that more babies than these are dying of malnutrition in the poor countries of the world; that Christians, Muslims, and Jews are killing each other in Lebanon, Palestine, and throughout the Middle East; that Orthodox, Catholics, Muslims, and Communists are dying every day in the Balkans.

I know that in Africa, in the Kashmir, in other parts

of India, bombs are frequently exploding. In the Sudan, northern Muslims are killing black Christians for the sake of the oil that is produced in the southern part of the country. Catholics and Protestants are murdering each other in civilized Ireland and England.

I've been to Haiti eleven times. Unemployment there is about seventy percent right now. How would Cincinnati exist with seventy percent unemployment? The average wage for those working in Haiti is less than three dollars a day. How do single mothers with two or three children feed their families on such meager incomes? How do they buy aspirins for sick babies?

And what are the problems among some of us Catholics in well-to-do Cincinnati? We quarrel about whether we should kneel or stand at Mass. We argue about what is "sacred space." We fight about where to place the tabernacle in our churches so that we can tell our Lord in the Blessed Sacrament that we love him and that we are praying for peace and unity in his world. Some of us say that those who don't agree with us no longer believe in the Real Presence. How do we know what they believe?

Some of us condemn our Archbishop, and any number of good, dedicated priests, for their honest, educated efforts at architectural and liturgical reform.

Conflict among us humans is common. Sometimes conflict is necessary. Sometimes it serves a good purpose. Honest discussion can help us arrive at consensus and truth.

But I suspect, after many years of living, that most

conflict is selfish. We all have our own desires and opinions and most of us don't often want to bow to the views of others. What does a pastor do if his parish is divided 51/49 percent, or 80/20 percent, over a proposed pastoral change? Some pastors I know aren't suggesting changes any more.

Millions are dying in our world over ethnic, political, and religious conflicts. And we Cincinnatians have the luxury of arguing about whether or not it is better to bow or genuflect.

Is Jesus weeping over Cincinnati? What do you think?

(Rev.) Joseph Beckmann

True reverence in the scriptural sense can heal both society and Church if and when the focus is on living the Mass and not on liturgical preferences rooted in a Western European culture. Let us learn from the life of our young adults like Julie Kalker!

DOORWAY THREE

Real Presence

Before we can discover the real presence of Christ in the breaking of the bread, we must discover how to be present to him. To learn how to be present to Christ is the doorway into his presence. God is always present to us. If we are far away, we cannot experience God's loving presence. Take a stereotypical experience between marriage partners. The wife may be lovingly present to her husband. She may be saying and doing something really important for him. Yet, he may not notice because something on TV or in the newspaper occupies his attention. Although she is present to him, he has not entered into her presence. The same can happen in our relationship with Christ. We must discover how to be present. There are two ways we learn how to be present to God: 1) learn to pray from the heart, and 2) learn how to be present to those around us. If we can learn how to be thus present on a daily basis, then we can learn how to be present to Christ in the Eucharist. We will be able to enter into his presence in the breaking of the bread.

First, we learn to be present by learning how to pray from the heart. During retreats and days of reflection one may hear thoughts on prayer from the heart based on the lived experience of the two thousand-year-old Christian community. Over the years, my spiritual journal has been filled with various phrases and words of wisdom taken from various retreats and spiritual directors. Here are some examples:

- Prayer is the breath of the soul. What happens when one stops breathing?
- Dedicate time to God. In prayer with the heart, you shall encounter God.
- By means of prayer, you shall obtain joy and peace.
- Don't just get prayer in, get into your prayer.
- Let prayer begin to rule in the whole world. Then our hearts will be richer because God will rule in the hearts of all.
- In prayer, you shall perceive the greatest joy and the way out of situations that has no exit.
- We are called to more active prayer and attendance at Holy Mass so that Mass will be an experience of God.
- Wake up to yourselves. Take time to meet with God in Church. Take time to meet among yourselves for family prayer or communal prayer and implore the grace of God.
- Decide for God, and from day to day, discover his will in prayer.

- Open yourself to God and surrender all your difficulties and crosses so God may turn everything into joy.
- You cannot open yourselves to God if you do not pray.
- Your days will *not* be the same regardless of whether you pray or not.

It becomes obvious that prayer is essential in order to be present to the One who loves us. Can this love be boring? If prayer is boring, it is because we are not praying from the heart, we are not yet present to the Lord who is present to us. Prayer is not a matter of time, but of love. We find time for what or who we love. The best way to learn prayer from the heart is to dedicate a time to God each day and start today. Begin with gratitude for the littlest gifts in your life or begin with an act of forgiveness.

Forgiveness is a powerful way to begin prayer from the heart, especially in a world where hearts are so filled with hurt and anger. One example of this is a parish in Croatia which had been divided. Some of the people had not talked to each other for generations. There were fights over the land, and some family members had married Moslem or Serbian spouses which increased suspicions and bitter hatred. Finally, one Sunday, a Franciscan missionary told the people that Mass would not begin until there was forgiveness. The people sat there in a tense silence. Finally, one man stood up and said, "I forgive them, now you forgive me." One by one, people followed and did the same. "I forgive her, now forgive me." It was the best experience of prayer and Eucharist the people in that small village had ever experienced. They truly learned to pray from the heart. When we learn to be present to God by prayer from the heart, then we can experience God's presence to us in the Eucharist.

When we love God first in prayer, then we will be able to recognize and love God in every person as God loves us. The second way we learn to become present to Christ is to be present to people we encounter daily. The monks in Gethsemane, a Trappist Monastery in Kentucky, sit on either side of the chapel, facing one another. Facing each other during the liturgy has a good reason: It is easy to find God's presence in creation, like bread and wine, but facing one another during the Eucharist is a way to find Christ's presence in others.

To be present to another is no easy task, but we learn to become more present to Christ in others and in prayer from the heart. This enables us to experience more fully the Real Presence in the Eucharist. What is an experience of the Real Presence? How can we explain it? It is the deepest experience of the entire Bible. The eucharistic words of Jesus, "This is my body" and "this is my blood," are found in all four gospels (see Mark 14:22-24, Luke 22:19-20, Matthew 26:26-28, John 6). Jesus' life, mercy, transfigured humanity, and divinity are eternally present to us in the Eucharist. When we enter Christ's presence we are taken up into a new reality. Thomas Aquinas says it this way: "It is not that the bread has become a new kind of thing in this world: it now belongs to a new world" (*Summa Theologica* Vol 58, 220).

To what can we liken the encounter with this new world and new love? It can be likened to our daily relationships, which we express through our own flesh and blood. Consider a father who leaves work early on a weekday, drives five hours to another city to be present at his son's college basketball game, and then drives home the same night. The father arrives home about 5:00 a.m., catches an hour of sleep, then goes to work. He does this often. Perhaps it would be enough to tell his son over the phone that he is thinking about him and cheering and praying for him. But think how much more it means to the child that his father is not just there in spirit—he is there in flesh. He is providing a *real presence* for his son. What a big difference!

A flesh-and-blood relationship can make a difference. Consider the story of an infant who lost both parents in a fire. The child became so traumatized that he clung to himself, arms crossed over his chest, as stiff as a board. When rescuers took the child to the hospital, he was placed in a crib just outside the nurses' station. Whenever the nurses and nurse's aides walked by, they would speak softly to the baby and gently caress him. Over a period of time, the baby began to respond. First a finger loosened, then a hand, then an arm, then a leg, until the baby was completely relaxed and finally recovered from the shock. The body-and-blood relationship with the nurses gradually brought about the child's wellness. Again, what a difference the *real presence* of these nurses made to the child. There's no substitute for a real flesh-and-blood relationship. The Spirit dwells in us so we might experience God, who wants a real relationship with us. Like the little baby in the nurses' station, we need a body-and-blood relationship with God in Christ. Yet where do we learn about body-and-blood relationships? We can only begin to understand the body and blood of Jesus when we understand true love in relationships involving friends, family, and marriage.

When we hear about body and blood as sacrifice, as in the sacrifice of the Mass, we think somebody or something has been killed. But in the scriptural worldview, the thought of blood is the presence of life. Sacrifice means communion of life. This brings to mind the wonderful image of an infant in the mother's womb. The infant is being nourished through the umbilical cord by the body and blood of the mother. It's not a violent act—the baby is receiving life. The mother's body is making all kinds of changes and sacrifices for the infant in her womb. But the mother is not thinking, "Oh, my body is making all kinds of sacrifices for the infant in my womb." Instead, the mother is very conscious of the communion she has with her infant, a communion of life. This relationship is truly a body-and-blood relationship. In a loving communion between the mother and the infant, that strong body-and-blood presence assures the child that the one the child most desires does in fact desire him or her. The bond between us and God, our loving parent, is just as strong and concrete. God wants a body-and-blood relationship with us. And as God's infants, we need that relationship. In the body-and-blood presence of Christ, we are assured that the One we most desire does in fact desire us.

The bread and wine are not simply *like* the body and blood of Christ; they *are* the body-and-blood presence of Christ. This is because our relationship is that concrete, that real, that wonderful! Jesus is God revealing God's self to us.

We can increase our understanding of God's presence during the eucharistic prayer and communion rite by thinking about being in the womb of God where we are fed concretely through the "umbilical cord" of the Holy Spirit. "This is my body which will be given up for you." "This is my blood, the blood of the new and everlasting covenant." Through these words of life, love, and communion, we encounter the person of Christ! There is no doubt that a body-and-blood relationship exists between a mother and her child. But they don't think of each other as body and blood. They think about the human relationship between them, whether or not it is mutually loving. It's the same way in the celebration of the Eucharist. We have a body-and-blood relationship with God in Christ. In this encounter, we no longer get stuck on the elements of bread and wine, body and blood. This is because we experience persons instead of things, relationships instead of magic. Respect for the body and blood of

Christ has to be for the person of Christ and for all people for whom he died—the two are inseparable. That is why we all, as a people, are called the *body of Christ*.

We cannot have respect for the body and blood of Christ—the person of Christ—if we knock down those for whom he died out of love. It is simple: We must have respect for one another. Can a man say he loves his wife if he abuses their children? Are not the children part of her? We cannot abuse one another, cannot help but want a community of compassion, mercy, peace, and justice, if we recognize that we all come from the same womb of God, the love of God poured out into our hearts through the outpouring of the Spirit; signed and sealed in the body-and-blood relationship we have in Christ. Indeed, the Eucharist is a real interpersonal encounter between God and the worshiping community precisely because Christ is body-and-blood present. Our human experience of love and relationships tell us that any lover seeks concrete union with the beloved. It is like the love between a mother and her infant in the womb. It is the love of God in Christ for his people not yet fully born into the reign of God: "…the bread that I will give for the life of the world is my flesh.…Very truly, I tell you, unless you eat the flesh of the Son of Man and drink his blood, you have no life in you.…Those who eat my flesh and drink my blood abide in me, and I in them" (John 6:51-56).

The Holy Spirit Is Our Doorkeeper

The purpose of these reflections is not so much to get more out of Mass as to get more into it. Everything up to this point has been to help us connect everyday life and the Eucharist. At the heart of all our troubles, relationships, and human presence is no longer a completely hopeless situation, a dead-end or a "no exit" sign. No, instead of walls, there are doorways. It is the Holy Spirit who opens all the doorways for us.

We have looked at three such doorways:

Our Pain

We have someone in whom our pain can be transformed from death into life in the paschal mystery. The eucharistic gathering is where pain can be transformed, not transferred, just as the grape crushed becomes something better. We can consciously live our pain in union with Jesus in the paschal mystery. The Eucharist will slowly begin to transform pain and death into life. "Slowly" is a key word, because the love revealed in the paschal mystery is not a quick fix; it takes time and our participation. We do this together and not alone around the Lord's table.

Our Relationships

Real reverence is how we treat people before we come to the eucharistic table and after we leave—reverence comes from truly living the Eucharist.

If we live the Eucharist, its reconciling and transforming grace in our relationships, and lay down our life in service to all Monday through Saturday, on Sunday we will more fully experience the love of the one who laid down his life for us.

Our Presence

Nothing happens without our presence. We do not allow someone to be present to us if we aren't present to them. God's presence is with us always but cannot reach us if we don't make ourselves present to God. When we learn to be present to God by prayer from the heart and present to Christ in others, then the real presence in the Eucharist will touch us.

Behind each of these doorways is grace. In the word "Eucharist" we find "charis," which in Greek means favor or grace. Eucharist is grace (charis). God really is our friend and doesn't ask much of us, only our surrender to grace. The Holy Spirit helps us to live a life of grace. "Amen" means "let it be so" in Hebrew, and in pronouncing it, we say yes to grace. Whenever we surrender to grace in our daily encounters, ups and downs, etc., our daily "amen" is connected to every "amen" we pray at Mass. We are continuing the Eucharist throughout the week as well as preparing for the next Eucharist. By the working of the Holy Spirit, we begin to live from grace to grace and Eucharist to Eucharist. The doorways open when we allow the Holy Spirit to make the connections.

Our everyday experiences need not be dramatic (intensely good or bad) for the Holy Spirit to work. With the Holy Spirit, with our daily surrender to grace, every word in the Eucharist connects with everyday life. As you read these examples, ask the Holy Spirit to help you to begin to make these life-giving connections for yourself. Looking at the scriptural and Jewish roots of these words, we can see more easily the connections:

In our Jewish roots, silence is praise. Therese, a tired mother, feels the soft skin of her baby, and in the silence of her heart she acknowledges the wonderful creation of God. Don builds an addition on to his house, and in the silence of his heart ponders how God must have built the universe! Vicky, a teenager, prays the rosary with her grandmother at home and in the silence of meditation comes to experience Jesus who is alive, not dead. During the response at Mass, "It is right to give him thanks and praise," Therese, Don, and Vicky are connecting and experiencing the living Jesus at Mass, because of the silent praise they offered throughout the week.

In Jewish thought, worship is an inner agreement with God. Following a high school retreat, a freshman in college decided to pray for agreement with God's will everyday. He prayed boldly: "What do you want me to do with my life?" He thought that if he just tried to do God's will daily, then he would slowly come to see what God's plan is for his entire life. Daily he would recite the prayer of the Trappist monk, Thomas Merton:

My Lord God, I have no idea where I am going, I do not see the road ahead of me. I cannot know for certain where it will end. Nor do I really know myself, and the fact that I think I am following your will does not mean that I am actually doing so. But I believe that the desire to please you does in fact please you. And I hope I have that desire in all that I am doing. I hope that I will never do anything apart from that desire. And I know that if I do this, you will lead me by the right road though I may know nothing about it. Therefore will I trust you always though I may seem to be lost and in the shadow of death. I will not fear, for you are ever with me, and you will never leave me to face my perils alone. Amen

FROM *THOUGHTS IN SOLITUDE*

How well this connects us to the Lord's Prayer, "Your will be done, on earth as it is in heaven," as well as to the Second Eucharistic Prayer, "…and all your saints who have done your will throughout the ages."

At Mass, we pray these words over the gifts:

"Blessed are you, Lord, God of all creation. Through your goodness we have this bread to offer, which earth has given and human hands have made. It will become for us the bread of life."

In the Jewish sense, "blessed be God" means "may there be more of God in this place." For us, as Christians, it means to discover Christ's presence where we thought we never would.

I remember a eucharistic minister in a parish who for personal reasons said he would visit just about any sick person except persons with AIDS. The day came when he got that call from a friend to come visit a family whose son was dying after having contracted AIDS from unprotected, casual sexual encounters. He reluctantly went because of his friend. One day, the eucharistic minister was there when the son asked his mother: "Why Mom, why me?" The mother looked at him and said, "I don't know; all I know is that you are my son, and I don't look at you from the waist down."

The eucharistic minister began to see how Mother Teresa could minister to AIDS patients, and how she brought them a merciful invitation to peace with God rather than an negative stereotype. The words at Mass, "Lord have mercy" and "Blessed be God," seem to come alive for him now. "Blessed be God" now means to him: "May there be more of God in this place where I bring communion, the bread of life, to people who feel abandoned by society—a place I never thought I'd ever go."

An experience with family, RCIA, or small Christian communities or prayer groups can help us connect to the Sunday assembly or gathering of people. In the Jewish sense, it is not simply being an individual which completes us, nor in being isolated, but being part of a people. Jan and Phil are in the RCIA. They experience a different view of "Church" and "Mass" through their small group experience one evening a week. I compare it to the experience I had in relationship with my father. Through our relationship, he gave me an experience which wholly differed from the concept of "Church" and "Mass" as cold, monotonous, and bureaucratic organized religion. It is reflected in my funeral homily for my dad. As you read it, pray to the Holy Spirit to help you connect with someone whose relationship with you made the gathering at the Lord's table a whole new experience.

Funeral Homily for My Dad

Perhaps this Thursday morning, February 24, it would be helpful for us to keep in mind the bigger picture—the Kingdom of Heaven. Did you ever notice how many

Kingdom of Heaven stories in the Scriptures involve food: "The Kingdom of God may be likened to a king who held a wedding feast"; or like today's gospel, where there is the experience of God's love in Jesus' multiplication of the loaves and fishes. If Jesus would ever have said that the reign of God is like a man who sold all he had and went out to buy a giant Hershey™ chocolate bar, Dad would have been the greatest martyr for the cause. Some people think that first you die, and then you share in the heavenly banquet. But to eat at the heavenly banquet table really means to begin to live the life of heaven on earth, live God's word now, until you reap its benefits forever. I would say it this way: Heaven grew in Dad until he grew into heaven when he closed his eyes for the last time, this past Saturday at 4 p.m.

So this morning, we might get in touch with the bigger picture of reality, the Kingdom of Heaven through this morning's gospel food story…compliments of Dad.

In the first part of the gospel, there is divine comedy or humor. After having told the disciples not to take any food along earlier that day, Jesus now tells the disciples to feed the crowd in the desert. It would be like me inviting every one of you out for dinner and then saying: "Oh, I forgot my wallet!" Divine comedy in the midst of tragedy. Aristotle, the philosopher, said that the ability to laugh is what separates us from animals. The Greek Orthodox begin their Easter celebration with a joke. Easter in the midst of Good Friday.

With Dad came the experiences of divine comedy. When Dad was in the seminary, just after World War II, he was asked by his professor who Melchizedek was. He got up and said: "Wasn't he the flautist for the Cincinnati Philharmonic Orchestra?" Word got back to the bishop. He wasn't amused. Dad wasn't long for the seminary. Later in life, when Dad suffered from Alzheimer's, I asked him who his guardian angel was. He answered, "Lucifer!" with a great big smile.

But divine comedy or joy in the Kingdom went deeper than just a sense of humor. Dad wrote, in a poem after the war, "Learn to smile even in heart-scourging trials." It is the joy expressed in the first reading: "For you shall go out in joy, and be led back in peace; the mountains and the hills before you shall burst into song" (Isaiah 55:12).

Divine comedy in tragedy, Easter in the midst of Good Friday, food in the desert, the Kingdom of Heaven growing in Dad until he grew into heaven.

The gospel story quickly moves on! Notice how the heart of Jesus was moved to pity for the crowd. Someone once said the real miracle wasn't the multiplication of the bread and fish, but the increase of compassion in the disciples who began to help serve the food. The Letter to the Philippians says it another way: "Rejoice. Let your gentleness be known to everyone. The Lord is near" (4:4-5). We experienced the Kingdom of unselfishness in Dad. Since he converted the garage of our home into his public accountant office, we kids got to witness every kind of person from every kind of economic status walk through those doors. One poor woman from down on the farm could not afford to pay money for Dad's services, so she left duck eggs. There were many others trapped in the mergers here in Northern Kentucky. What do you do if you are fifty-plus-years-old, worked loyally for one place for twenty-six years, and now have to start over? For every five minutes Dad took to get the necessary figures from his clients, he spent fifty-five minutes attending to their wounded minds and broken spirits. Dad showed us that the Church exists not to serve itself but to serve the world. However, on the other side of the door in our home was an even more incredible concern. For instance, when Dad found out he had diabetes and Alzheimer's, his first response was: "This isn't something the kids will get, is it?" He had just been handed the news about what will eventually take his life, and his only concern was how it would affect us.

Another example comes from the golf course. I had hit the ball straight over four fairways in the wrong direction, and Dad was already on his way, getting the ball to save me the humiliation.

Hanging in the hallway of our home was a crucifix, a great symbol of the mysterious compassion of God. Dad was intrigued by a show on the history channel about a Jewish boy in the 1930s who had a friend who was Catholic. When he would visit his friend, he noticed a crucifix on the wall and would think it strange. After the war and the holocaust, this Jewish boy became rabbi of the synagogue in Rome. He still remembered the cross from his childhood. He now saw the cross not as the story of Job who had no choice but to suffer; but more like the servant in Isaiah who freely took on the burdens of the people.

Dad freely gave it all. Compassion has reasons which reason does not know: the Kingdom of compassion—heaven growing in Dad until Dad grew into heaven.

Finally, there is the climax of the story. Jesus gives thanks. Thanksgiving is a way of life in the Hebrew Scriptures. It is an attitude directly opposed to "the world owes me" or "I didn't ask to be born into this life." It is a response in gratitude to life itself, no matter how bad it may seem at times. Even painful situations become an opportunity to love God and love people in gratitude for the gift of life.

We are very grateful. I don't know how much you know about Alzheimer's, but sometimes a person can become violent and hostile. Dad was spared that part of the disease. Mom labored twenty-four hours a day, along with great help from hospice and home care. And each family member did what he or she could whenever possible. We are so grateful that Dad died at home and in peace. At this point in the liturgy, gratitude begins to replace any false guilt that is associated with the grieving process. Around the banquet table of the bread of life, Dad is with us always, in the kingdom of divine comedy, the kingdom of compassion. and the kingdom of eternal gratitude…the Kingdom of Heaven growing in us until we grow into heaven. That is the bigger reality, the bigger picture for all of us.

From the homily, I hope it is clear how much my father's life and death lead me to a deeper experience of "Mass" and "Church." Walking with the people of God and experiencing the Holy Spirit working in family, friendship, or small group experiences like the RCIA, prayer groups, youth groups, young adult ministry, Cursillo, etc., can give us a better taste of "Church" and "Mass" gathered together at the table of the bread of life.

Hopefully, through this little reflection on the Eucharist, a person can begin to see how he or she can allow the deep gift of God's love in the eucharistic gathering to come alive. As Jesus said, "I came that [you] may have life, and have it abundantly" (John 10:10). We have so much more reason to give thanks to God both now and forever in heaven. Eucharist is thanksgiving!

In closing, we are left with a simple invitation to pray to the Holy Spirit each day and especially before each eucharistic celebration: "Come Holy Spirit!"

ADDENDUM

A Few Common Questions from Youth and Young Adults

Q. Do all the fancy vestments and chalices make the liturgy better?

A. When we are dealing with the Eucharist, we are dealing with God's greatest gift of love. So we want to use what is respectful of that gift. However, it is always our hearts open to conversion, not fancy garments and chalices, which make the liturgy better and more respectful. Good Eucharist makes good liturgy, not vice versa.

Q. Why do people put all that money into church buildings and art? What about the poor?

A. Scripture says, "It is written, 'My house shall be a house of prayer'" (Luke 19:46). Certainly, we need to maintain structures which express that. The artwork can help awaken the human spirit to much more. If you go to the Sacred Heart Church on the campus of the University Notre Dame, Indiana, you'll find a sculpture of the prodigal son with his father. It has moved many a person to seek reconciliation and unity. However, there needs to be simplicity, especially in a world where we like to make our lives so complicated. The Trappist Abbey at Gethsemane in Kentucky is beautiful in this way. It reflects a certain simplicity and poverty to remind us of our poverty before God and the poverty of the human spirit in the world hungering for God's love. This kind of simplicity might lead us to do more for the poor. There ought to be a preferential option for the poor in all our financial decisions.

Q. What about multicultural Masses?

A. With the Internet, we live more and more in a global society. It makes sense that Masses are more or less multicultural and bilingual, depending on the needs where you live. If you live in a multicultural parish, however, the ideal would be to get different ethnic groups working together outside the liturgy in various parish activities and ministries, in order to open dialogue and break down barriers. Only then do you begin to look at the liturgy itself. The question each person and each ethnic group must ask is not, "How can I make the liturgy better for me?" but "What is in it for all of us (universally)?"

Q. What about youth at the Sunday Mass?

A. Parents and grandparents have tried so hard to pass on the beautiful gift of Eucharist. The community can help by offering this preferential sensitivity toward youth and young adults. I humbly think all the Sunday liturgies ought to reflect not only a preferential option for the poor, but a preferential option for the teenager and young adult.

Q. How should we dress for Mass?

A. From the inside out! How is our mind and heart clothed? As Saint Paul says, "As God's chosen ones, holy and beloved, clothe yourselves with compassion, kindness, humility, meekness, and patience" (Colossians 3:12).

Q. Should parents make us go to Mass?

A. Hopefully, parish, parents, and youth can work together so that we can all find reason to want to go. Parents lead best by example, not by words or arguments. If we love God first, it will be easy to come. The reflection we have shared in this booklet can help parents as well as youth to want to come. The Mass is really never boring! We need to learn how to enter into this great gift of grace and love. There are many ways to involve youth and young adults in the liturgy as well. Ask Mary, the Mother of Jesus, to pray with you and your family for the outpouring of the Holy Spirit upon you and our world. The Holy Spirit makes all things new.